Weather Watchers

Snow

Cassie Mayer

Heinemann
LIBRARY

www.heinemann.co.uk/library

Visit our website to find out more information about **Heinemann Library** books.

To order:

☎ Phone 44 (0) 1865 888066

🖷 Send a fax to 44 (0) 1865 314091

🖥 Visit the Heinemann Bookshop at www.heinemann.co.uk/library to browse our catalogue and order online.

First published in Great Britain by Heinemann Library, Halley Court, Jordan Hill, Oxford OX2 8EJ, part of Harcourt Education. Heinemann is a registered trademark of Harcourt Education Ltd.

Editorial: Tracey Crawford, Cassie Mayer, Dan Nunn, and Sarah Chappelow
Design: Jo Hinton-Malivoire
Picture Research: Tracy Cummins, Tracey Engel, and Ruth Blair
Production: Duncan Gilbert

Originated by Chroma Graphics (Overseas) Pte. Ltd
Printed and bound in China by South China Printing Company

10 digit ISBN 0 431 18257 4
13 digit ISBN 978 0 431 18257 5

11 10 09 08 07
10 9 8 7 6 5 4 3 2 1

British Library Cataloguing in Publication Data
Mayer, Cassie
    Snow. - (Weather watchers)
    1.Snow - Juvenile literature
    I.Title
    551.5'784
A full catalogue record for this book is available from the British Library.

Acknowledgements
The publishers would like to thank the following for permission to reproduce photographs: Corbis pp. **4** (cloud; sunshine, G. Schuster/zefa; rain, Anthony Redpath), **7** (Matthias Kulka), **8** (Craig Tuttle), **15** (Jonathan Blair), **16** (Grafton Marshall Smith), **17** (Jeff Albertson), **20** (Darrell Gulin), **23** (snowflake, Matthias Kulka; blizzard, Grafton Marshall Smith); Getty Images pp. **4** (lightning; snow, Marc Wilson Photography), **5** (Marc Wilson Photography), **6** (Chris Hackett), **9** (Kennan Harvey), **14** (Yuri Dojc), **19** (Michael Dunning), **21** (Brian Bailey), **23** (water vapor, Kennan Harvey); Photo Researchers, Inc. p. **18** (B. & C. Alexander).

Cover photograph reproduced with permission of Getty Images (Stone/Christoph Burki). Back cover photograph reproduced with permission of Getty Images (Brian Bailey).

Every effort has been made to contact copyright holders of any material reproduced in this book. Any omissions will be rectified in subsequent printings if notice is given to the publishers.

Contents

What is weather?

There are many types of weather.
Weather changes all the time.

Snow is a type of weather.

What is snow?

Snow is pieces of frozen water.

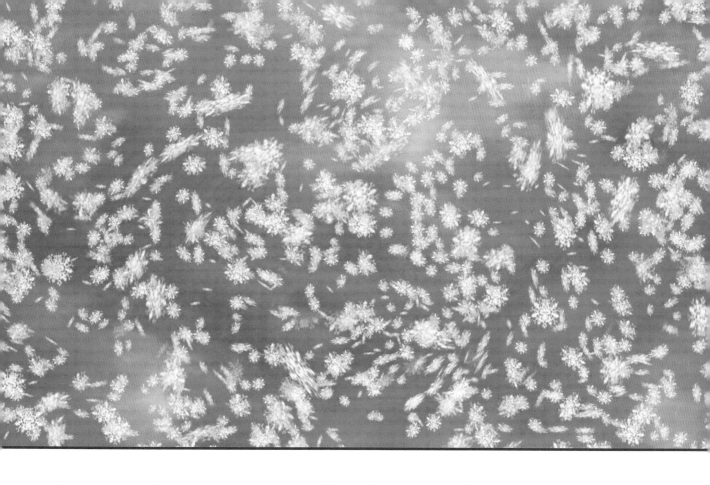

These pieces are called snowflakes.
Snow falls from clouds when it is cold.

water vapour

Snowflakes are made from water vapour. Water vapour is air that is full of moisture.

Water vapour comes from living things.

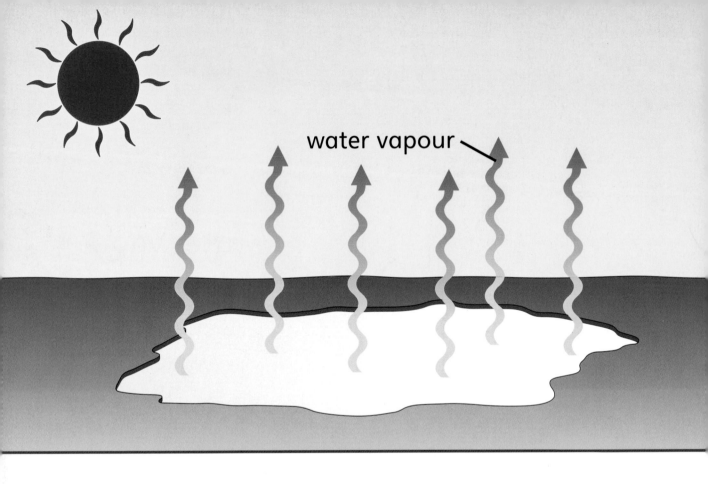

Water vapour rises into the air.
As it cools it forms water droplets.

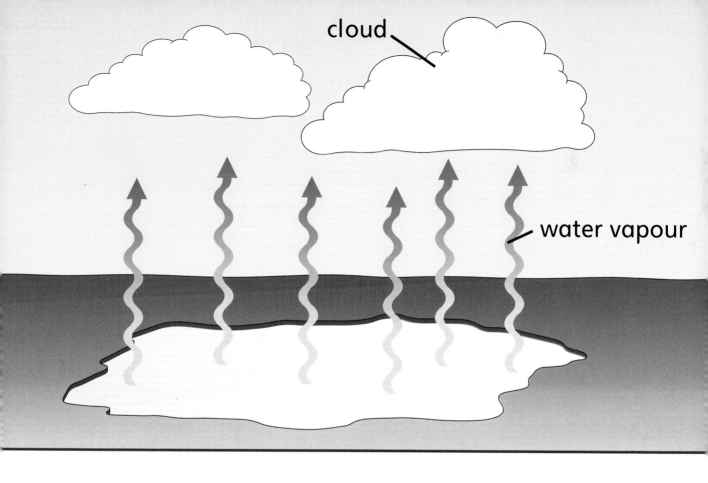

cloud

water vapour

These droplets form clouds.

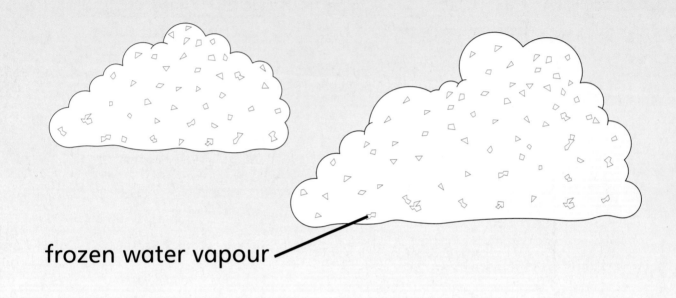

frozen water vapour

If it is very cold, water vapour freezes in the clouds.

snowflake

Then water vapour forms snowflakes.
The snowflakes fall from the cloud.

13

Types of snow

When wet snowflakes stick together it is called heavy snow.

When it is very cold the snowflakes do not stick together. This is called light snow.

When there is a heavy snowfall and strong winds it is called a blizzard.

Blizzards can make driving very difficult.

Snow around the world

Some places get a lot of snow.

Some places get no snow.

How does snow help us?

Living things need water to grow.
Snow brings water back to the earth.

Snowy days can be fun!

What to wear when it snows

hat

scarf

coat

gloves

trousers

boots

Picture glossary

blizzard a big snowstorm with strong winds

snowflake a tiny piece of frozen water. Snowflakes fall from clouds.

water vapour part of the air outside

Index

Notes to parents and teachers
Before reading
Talk about different weather. Ask the children which type of weather they like best. Talk about when it snows. What do they like to do?

After reading
Sing the song to the tune of "Frere Jacques": Dance like snowflakes (x2) In the air (x2) Whirling, twirling, snowflakes (x2) Here and there.
Make a snowflake: Fold a square piece of paper in half three times. Cut each folded corner and make different shaped cuts around the edges. Open out the snowflake and suspend from the ceiling.
Watch the "Snowman dance" from the DVD *The Snowman* by Raymond Briggs.

Titles in the *Weather Watchers* series include:

Hardback 0 431 18258 2

Hardback 0 431 18256 6

Hardback 0 431 18257 4

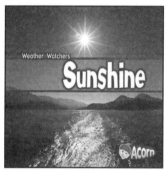

Hardback 0 431 18259 0

Hardback 0 431 18255 8

Hardback 0 431 18260 4

Find out about other titles from Heinemann Library on our website www.heinemann.co.uk/library